Pray This Way

Lola Granola

WestBow Press books may be ordered through booksellers or by contacting:

WestBow Press
A Division of Thomas Nelson & Zondervan
1663 Liberty Drive
Bloomington, IN 47403
www.westbowpress.com
844-714-3454

Because of the dynamic nature of the Internet, any web addresses or links contained in this book may have changed since publication and may no longer be valid. The views expressed in this work are solely those of the author and do not necessarily reflect the views of the publisher, and the publisher hereby disclaims any responsibility for them.

Any people depicted in stock imagery provided by Getty Images are models, and such images are being used for illustrative purposes only. Certain stock imagery © Getty Images.

Scripture taken from the King James Version of the Bible.

ISBN: 978-1-6642-8035-9 (sc)
ISBN: 978-1-6642-8036-6 (e)

Library of Congress Control Number: 2022918652

Print information available on the last page.

WestBow Press rev. date: 11/07/2022

For Harper, Dozier, Bennett, Vivvie, Rhodes, Brewer, Ellie Barnes, Hastings, Manning and all of my grands yet to come. I am cheering you on as you grow in Jesus.

Prayer

Harken unto the voice of my cry, my King and my God: for to you I will pray.

My voice shalt thou hear in the morning, O Lord; in the morning will I direct my prayer unto thee, and I will look up.

Psalms 5:2-3 KJV

Pray, Pray, Pray all Day.
Pray, Pray, Even When You Play.

Pray By Yourself.
Pray With A Friend.

Pray With Your Mom.

Pray With
Your Dad.

Pray When You Are Happy.

Pray When You Are Sad.

Hey, Hey,
You Can Even Pray
When You Are Mad.

Pray When You
Are Worried.

Pray When You Are Hurried.

Pray In The Morning
When The Sun Comes Up.

Pray, Pray,
With Your
Favorite Pup.

Pray, Pray, Pray at Noon.

Pray, Pray, When You Will Eat Soon.

Pray, Pray,
When It's
Time For Bed.

Pray, Pray, When You
Lay Down Your Head.

Pray For
Yourself,
Pray For
Others.

16

Pray
For Your
Sisters,
Pray
For Your
Brothers.

Pray
When
You Are
Sick.

Pray
When You
Are Well.

Pray For Your Preacher.

Pray For Your Teacher.

Pray For Your Friends.
Pray For Your Neighbors.

You Can Even Pray For Those
Who Are Misbehavers.

It's The Greatest
Way To Talk
To Your
Heavenly Father,

Who, By The Way,
You Can Never Bother!

Pray, Pray, Pray Without Ceasing, Either Night Or Day.

God Is Only A Prayer Away.

Confess Your Sins When You Pray.
Say You Are Sorry When You Pray.
Ask Forgiveness When You Pray.
When You Pray, Thank God
For Your Blessings Every Day.

And If You Are Still Wondering
What To Say When You Pray,
Jesus Said "Pray This Way:"

Our Father, Who Art In Heaven,
Hallowed Be Thy Name.
Thy Kingdom Come.
Thy Will Be Done.
On Earth As It Is In Heaven.
Give Us This Day Our Daily Bread.
And Forgive Us Our Trespasses,
As We Forgive Those Who Trespass Against Us.
And Lead Us Not Into Temptation,
But Deliver Us From Evil.
For Thine Is The Kingdom,
And The Power,
And The Glory,
Forever And Ever.

Amen.

Matthew 6:9-13

Printed in the United States
by Baker & Taylor Publisher Services